Sweet Stan

by Lucy Floyd
illustrations by T. F. Cook

Harcourt Brace & Company

Orlando Atlanta Austin Boston San Francisco Chicago Dallas New York Toronto London

Stan was a sweet little whale. But Stan was afraid.

Stan stayed close to Mother.

One day Mother said,
"You swim well, Stan.
You must swim alone."

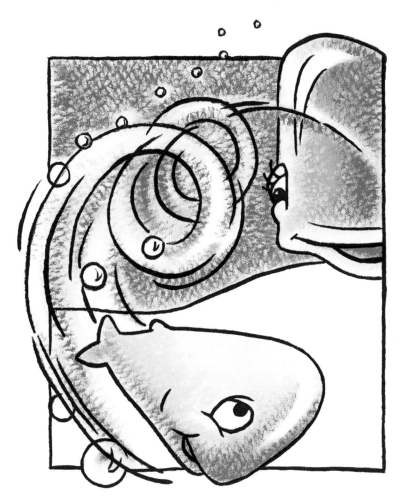

"You have skills, Stan.
You slosh, swish, and
spin!"

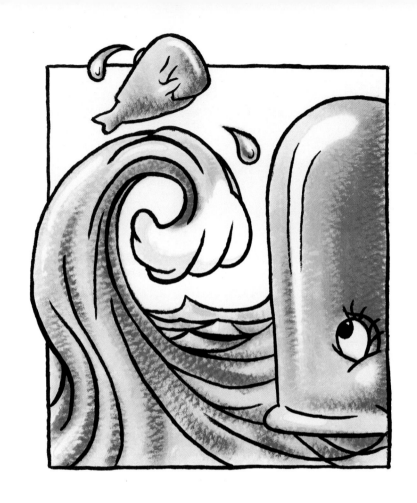

"You skip, skim, slip,
and slide over waves!"
Mother said.

"I can slosh, swish,
spin, skip, skim, slip,
slide, and swim with
you," Stan sniffed.

"I hate to scold," said
Mother. "You're my
sweet Stan. But you
8   must swim alone."

So Stan swam alone.
"You're doing swell,
Stan!" said Mother.
"Don't stop!" 9

"I swam alone!" Stan
said with a smile.

"I might never stop!
But may I still spend
the night with you?"

"Yes," Mother said
with a smile. "You're
still my sweet Stan!"